For Barb and all my little monsters
Alex, Lucy, Benny and Eddy
-TR

ISBN-13: 978-1481152914   ISBN-10: 1481152912

Visit us at:
www.MyVerySillyMonster.com

My Very Silly Monster ABCs
©2012 Tim Read / 5 Fingers Creative

My Very Silly

MONSTER
ABCs

by Tim Read

Alex's Amazing Apple

Benny's
Blue
Ball

Carl
Collects
Cans

Donald's Dandy Dancing

Eddy
Eats
Everything

Fred's
Fancy
Flying

Glenn's Green Glasses

Harry's
Huge
Hat

Ian's Invisible Ink

Junior Juggles Jelly Fish

Kim's Kooky Kiwi

Lucy
Loves
Lemonade

Mike's Magic Monkey

Nancy's
New
Necklace

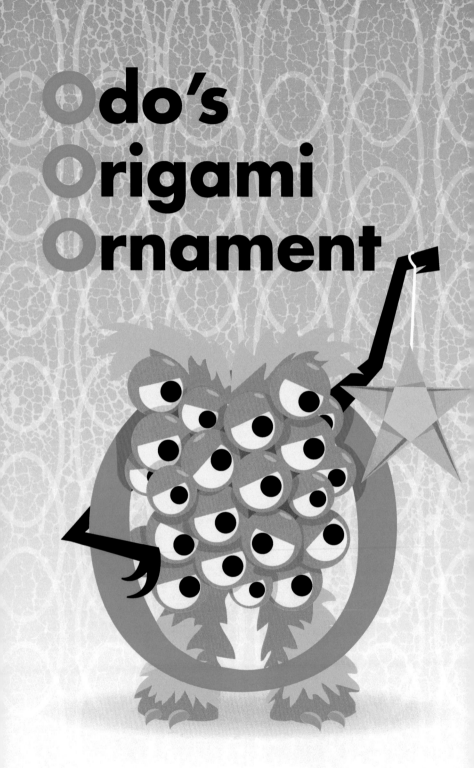

Odo's
Origami
Ornament

Polly's Purple Pickle

Quinn's Quality Quiche

Roberto's
Red
Radish

Sid Sings Sweetly

Tim's Tiny TuTu

Under
Unger's
Umbrella

Wanda
Wears
Waffles

Xing
X-rays
Xaria & Xiu

Yakov's Yodeling Yam

Zane's Zig Zag Zipper

Addy's
amasing
APPLY

Draw your own
ABC Monster
with the first letter
of your name!

Also available from

MY VERY
SILLY MONSTER

43885317R00020

Made in the USA
Middletown, DE
21 May 2017